Academic Advisement Program

for Grades 4-6

*Lessons, Activities, Games and Reproducible
Forms & Handouts to Help Students
Become More Successful in School*

by Lisa King, Ed.S., LPC

Cover Design by Amy Rule
Layout/graphics by Elaine Callahan
Project Supervisor - Susan Bowman
Project Editing - Susan Bowman

ISBN# 1-59850-003-1

Library of Congress
2005936308

10 9 8 7 6 5 4 3 2 1
Printed in the United States of America

youth light
inc.

P.O. Box 115
Chapin, South Carolina 29036
(800) 209-9774 • (803) 345-1070
Fax (803) 345-0888 • Email YL@sc.rr.com

Dedication

This book is dedicated to my parents....
who raised me well and always provided loving advisement.

Acknowledgements

A world of gratitude goes out to the following people who have supported this author in the writing of this book and beyond.

My sister Traci King, who is always supportive, encouraging, and just a phone call away.

My friends who are my sisters by choice.

Bob and Susan Bowman who have been the editing and publishing backbone of my endeavors.

My team of colleagues who helped me edit and fine tune this book: Lori Armbruster, Allison O'Neil, and Dawn Haskett.

Theodora Alam, RN for translating the parent permission slips into Spanish. This was a great help and a necessary part of the book that could not have been done without you!

The students and staff of Blackwell Elementary in Marietta, GA. They have been a community of encouragement and growth.

The counselors of Cobb County who continue to strive for excellence.

My parents, who deserve many mentions of thanks for a lifetime of unconditional love.

Table of Contents

Introduction and How to Use this Book

How much of your job involves working with students who are educationally at-risk? How are you as a counselor being an advocate for these students? What programs or interventions are you implementing? This program, *Academic Advisement for Grades 4-6*, was created out of the need for a more formal program to help unmotivated or underachieving students. Research shows that students are more likely to improve academically through a multi-faceted approach including involvement from parents, teachers, belief in oneself, and structured skill building (Brigman and Campbell, 2003). The program described here allows the counselor to facilitate academic improvement through a combination of individual and group guidance sessions.

This book presents a systemetic, chronological approach to running an academic advisement program. Each chapter gives a step-by-step description of what to do in each session. This program has been designed for use with individual and groups of students with 8-12 students in each group. However it can also be implemented with an entire classroom. Subsequently, counselors can gauge how to implement this program to best fit their school.

The first chapter in this book details what the counselor can do to prepare for this program. Next you will see the orientation chapter, which is a session where the students learn why they are in the group and defines group goals. You will find icebreakers, group activities as well as an outline for establishing individual goals within these pages. Throughout the book, the group and individual sessions are outlined with reproducible worksheets provided. Many of the worksheets make up the student workbook that can be created for each participating students. Please refer to page 2 for an outline of this program.

There is a continued need to help at-risk students, and counselors can implement this program as a way to bring a creative and data-driven intervention to their school. In the future it is the hope of this author to collect data to support the efficacy of this program. (Please email me with any data derived from using this program at kidscounseling@yahoo.com). We all know that programs that are research based are needed in the field of school counseling and I hope to have some of the research in the future editions of this book.

Outline of Program

Here is a step-by-step progression of Academic Advisement, which includes an orientation session, five group sessions and three individual sessions that make up this program.

STEP 1: The **counselor prepares** to implement the program. Details of how the counselor needs to get ready for this program are found in Chapter 1: Counselor Preparation for Advisement Program.

STEP 2: The counselor will facilitate a **group orientation session** for all members of the academic advisement program. Details are found in Chapter 2: Group Orientation.

STEP 3: The **first formal group session** will take place next. Each group session will have different content dependent on the group needs. All choices for lessons are included in Chapter 5: Small Group Content and Lesson Plans.

STEP 4: The counselor sets up **individual sessions** for each member that last about 15 minutes each. The information that describes this session is in Chapter 4: Individual Session One.

STEP 5: The **second group session** will take place next. Each group session will have content dependent on the group needs. All choices for lessons are included in Chapter 5: Small Group Content and Lesson Plans.

STEP 6: The **third group session** will take place next. Each group session will have different content dependent on the group needs. All choices for lessons are included in Chapter 5: Small Group Content and Lesson Plans.

STEP 7: The counselor sets up a **second individual session** for each member that last about 15 minutes each. The information that describes this session is in Chapter 6: Individual Session Two.

STEP 8: The **fourth group session** will take place next. Each group session will have content dependent on the group needs. All choices for lessons are included in Chapter 5: Small Group Content and Lesson Plans.

STEP 9: The fifth and **final group session** will take place next. This group session will have content that brings closure and evaluates growth. All choices for lessons are included in Chapter 7: Final Group Session.

STEP 10: The counselor sets up a third and **final individual session** for each member that last about 20 minutes. In this session, it is optional for the parent and/or teacher to be invited. Details for this session are found in Chapter 8: Final Individual Session.

Chapter 1:
Counselor Preparation
for Advisement Program

Overview:

In this chapter, counselors can see how to prepare for an academic advisement program.

Contents

Getting "Buy-In" from Administrators and Teachers

MEETING WITH ADMINISTRATION

Getting administrative support is a key part of successfully implementing this program.

When meeting with administrators,
make sure to cover these key points:

What is my idea?
How do I plan to implement it?
How will students change as a result of my program?

1

2

PRESENTING IDEA TO TEACHERS

Counselors should plan on meeting with teachers after getting administrative "buy-in." Before meeting with teachers you can send a letter explaining the program (page 6).

Date:

Dear Teachers and Administrators:

This letter is to introduce a new program I would like to offer as part of
_____'s *(Name of School)* developmental and comprehensive guidance program. One of the primary roles of a school counselor is to help alleviate obstacles that might be interfering with a child's academics. In order to further help with this issue, I am introducing a program called *Academic Advisement*.

This program will consist of group and individual sessions with selected students. Advisement will be implemented in a very similar manner as a typical small group counseling experience at school, with an addition of several individual appointments with students. Also, in Academic Advisement, data will be collected to track student improvement. The ultimate goal is student success. Parents and teachers will be made aware of the student's progress throughout the program. Topics discussed in Academic Advisement will be:

- **Motivation**
- **Goal Setting**
- **Learning Styles and Methods**
- **Procrastination**
- **Stress Management**
- **Organization**

I am very excited for the opportunity to work with these students. When the adults in a child's life work together to encourage a child to become motivated and engaged in academics, improvement is inevitable. I look forward to working toward our school's mission of academic success.

Please meet me briefly on _____ at _____ in
_____ where I will answer any questions.

Sincerely,

Selecting Students
for the Advisement Process

There are several options for selecting students for this program. Below are some issues to consider in selecting students for the academic advisement program.

KIDS WHO ARE IN SPECIAL EDUCATION

One thing to take into consideration is the issue of special education. While any student would benefit from the Academic Advisement Program, students receiving special education might not be given priority to participate unless the teacher or parent request this assistance. Why? Simply put, because they are already (or will soon be) receiving extra academic services to support them.

MARGINAL LEARNERS

Marginal learners, students who are slow learners, often do not qualify for special services, so this program might be used exclusively for that population. Of course the selection of students is up to the school. Data should drive the program, so counselors should do a needs-assessment, to determine what your school needs.

KIDS WHO HAVE ATTENDANCE ISSUES

Children who have chronic attendance issues might benefit from this program. These students might thrive in having a counselor paying positive attention to them. This might motivate them to come to school. Also the chronic absenteeism can be closely monitored by the counselor.

UNMOTIVATED STUDENTS

A student who is an underachiever or unmotivated might be a great candidate for the academic advisement program. Getting positive one to one attention from a counselor and also sharing feelings with peers about school might help to motivate this student. Also, the skills-building content of the group sessions address issues associated with motivation.

A List of Students to Consider

Teachers: Please use this chart to list students who you think would benefit from this program:

Student Name	# Failing Grades This Year	Standardized Test Score Reading	Standardized Test Score Math	Retained?	ESO/ELL	Special Ed?	Other Variable?

Counselors can select students for this group, or teachers can each decide on the most needy students with parameters given by the counselor.

Counselors:

Here is a memo for teachers to email or attach to the permission slips (page 9). Also suggest to teachers to make a copy in case they have to send a second copy home.

Teachers,

Please fill out the students strengths and concerns and then send the permission slip(s) home. You can return them to my box when you receive the permission slip(s) back.

Thanks!

Dear Parent/Guardian:

This letter is to explain to you a great opportunity for your child, _____.
Your child is invited to participate in an academic advisement program with the primary goal being to ensure that he/she achieves up to his/her potential. This program consists of group sessions to work on school success skills as well as individual sessions, which will allow for monitoring individual goals. Below is a recap of concerns and strengths your child's teacher is noticing. Please know that your involvement with academics is essential to helping your child achieve and I will be communicating with you about the things that your child can do to make this a successful year.

Student's Strengths:

Behavioral Concerns:

Academic Concerns:

I look forward to the opportunity to work with your child. Thanks for your support and call me if you have any questions!

Sincerely,

- -

PLEASE RETURN THIS TO YOUR CHILD'S TEACHER BY: _____

I give my child, _____, permission to participate in academic advisement.

I prefer that my child, _____, not participate in academic advisement.

_____   Date _____
Parent/Guardian Signature

PERMISSO DE PADRE

Estimado Padre/Guardian

      Esta carta es para explicarle una gran oportunidad para su hijo_____.
Su hijo esta invitado a participar en un programa de consejo académico con la primera
meta de asegurar que el/ella llegue a su potencial. Este programa consiste de sesiones de
grupo para trabajar en conocimientos escolares y sesiones individuales que vigilan metas
individuales. Sigue una lista de intereses y problemas que los maestros de su hijo estan
notando. Por favor, sepa que su envolvimiento con los estudios es esencial para ayudar a
su hijo triumfar y voy a estar comunicandome con usted sobre las cosas su hijo puede
hacer para triumfar este ano.

FUERZAS DEL ALUMNO:

PROBLEMAS DE COMPORTAMIENTO:

PROBLEMAS ACADÉMICOS:

Espero la oportunidad a trabajar con su hijo. Gracias por su apoyo y llameme si tiene
alguna pregunta.

Sinceramente,

_____

POR FAVOR REGRESE ESTE PERMISO AL MAESTRO DE SU HIJO ANTES_____

___ Doy permiso a mi hijo, _____ a participar en el Programa de
Consejo Académico.

___ Prefiero que mi hijo, _____ no participe en el Programa de
Consejo Academico

Firmo_____Padre/Guardian   Fecha: _____

Counselor Guide
for Student Workbooks

 To create the student workbook make copies of the following pages:
(Student workbook pages will be designated by an icon in the top corner of these pages.)

*Allow the students to decorate their own
workbook cover on page 12.*

_____'s

Student
Workbook

Orientation Invitations

Counselor: Copy these invitations and send one invitation to each student.

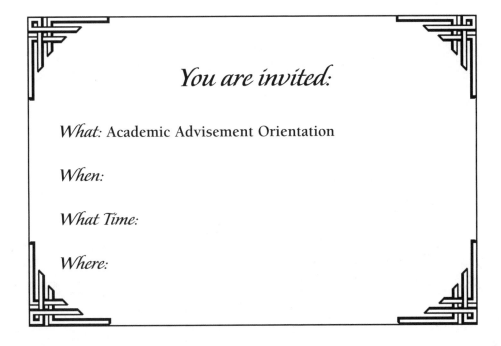

You are invited:

What: Academic Advisement Orientation

When:

What Time:

Where:

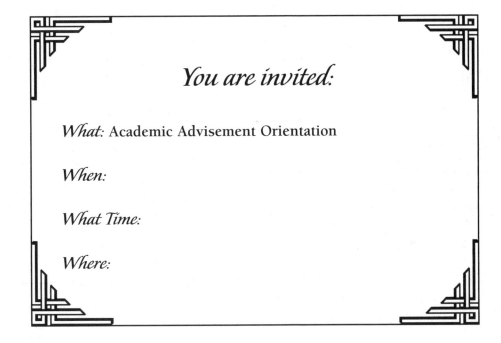

You are invited:

What: Academic Advisement Orientation

When:

What Time:

Where:

Chapter 2:
Group Orientation
for Academic Advisement

Overview:

The following items will be discussed in this orientation group session:

- Reasons for Being in This Program
- Rules of the Group
- Proposed Schedule of the Program
- Questions/Answer Session
- Initial Paperwork
- Student Notebooks will be Distributed

Before this session what does the counselor need to do?
- Send permission slips home to parents (see pg 9 or 10).
- Create notebooks for students (see pg 11).
- Send orientation invitations to students (see pg 13).
- Send page 25 to teachers to request student goals.

Time needed for this session: 30-45 minutes

Number of participants suggested: 8-12

After this session what does the counselor need to do?
- Send appointment cards for next group session (pg 29 or 30).

Contents

Academic Advisement Attendance

Student Name	Teacher Name	Orientation	Group	Individual	Group	Group	Individual	Group	Group	Individual	Group	Group	Individual

Orientation _____

Group _____

Individual Session _____

Group _____

Group _____

Individual Session _____

Group _____

Group _____

Individual Session _____

Group Orientation

Students will arrive for the orientation meeting. The counselor can implement the activities for this session in any order they wish, but should include all parts of the session that are suggested. The suggested progression of events is below. An agenda to distribute to students is on page 21.

Procedures:

1. Distribute Agendas to Students.

2. Introduction:
   - Counselor says, "Welcome to academic advisement. Before we get started why don't we all introduce ourselves. Let's go around the circle and say our name and the best vacation you've ever gone on."
   - Participants follow the directions.

3. Go Over Group Rules.
   - Display the rules (page 19) so that everyone can see them in the meeting area.
   - Read Group Rules together and explain as needed. Additionally reiterate that these rules are also in place during individual sessions. Consider the quote below when making rules for the group.

> *According to Sam Gladding (1994), "Counseling groups run best when the rules governing them are few and clear...Members should agree to keep each others' confidentiality, not attack each other verbally or physically, to actively participate in the group process, and to speak one at a time."*

4. Icebreaker Activity
   - Choose an icebreaker activity from Chapter 3.

5. Discuss Goal Setting (pages 25-27)

6. Discuss "Keeping Track of Group Points" (page 28)

7. Explain Counselor 'Check-In' Passes (page 24)

8. Distribute Notebooks (see page 11 for details)

9. Allow Students to Fill Out Questionnaire (page 22).

GROUP RULES

✔ Be active **LISTENERS.**

   (Let your body language show that you are listening!)

✔ Be **PUNCTUAL**

   (We start on time.)

✔ **RESPECT**

   (No put downs)

✔ Things we say are **CONFIDENTIAL.**

   (What is said in the group stays in the group.)

✔ You may pass your turn.

ANY QUESTIONS?

Ideas for Starting Each Group

ICEBREAKER FORMAT

For each group session, an icebreaker should be done to start the group. Why? Icebreakers are done as a warm up activity to ease tension, facilitate group bonding, and as a ritual to start the group session. There are many icebreakers to choose from in Chapter 3. The counselor can choose any of these icebreakers (or one of their own) to start each group session.

GETTING GROUP STARTED ON TIME

One idea to get students to come to group on-time is that everyone who gets to group on time gets an extra point (see page 27 for explanation of extra points). Also, everyone who is on time writes their name on a slip of paper and puts it in a designated basket. At the end of group, the counselor can draw one name from the on-time students to go to a treasure box or get a piece of candy. This serves as a positive reinforcement for kids getting to group on time and not wasting the precious few moments that academic advisement takes place.

Academic Advisement Orientation Agenda

1. Group Rules

2. Icebreaker

3. Why Are You Here?

4. A Collective Group Goal: Attendance

5. Choosing a Specific Individual Learning Goal

6. Counselor "Check-Ins"

7. Distribute Notebooks

8. Student Questionnaire

9. Discuss Individual Student Appointments

Academic Advisement Student Questionnaire

Name_____

What is your favorite subject in school?_____

What is your least favorite subject in school? _____

Are you satisfied with the grades you are now making? _____

How many elementary schools have you attended?_____

Are you absent a lot? If so, why? _____

Are you tardy a lot? If so, why? _____

Fill in the blanks in the following sentences.

School is _____

Paying attention is _____

I think my teacher is _____

My teacher thinks that I am _____

The things that are usually on my mind are about _____

My family thinks that I am _____

_____ likes to play with me because _____

At school I usually feel _____

One thing you should know about me is _____

At school I'd like to improve on_____

Put a 1 by things that are most important to you. Put a 2 by things that are second most important to you, and a 3 by what is third most important.

_____Being popular _____Getting along with family

_____Doing well in school _____Being good at sports

_____Wearing stylish clothes _____Staying out of trouble

_____Trying my best _____Sleeping

My counselor can share these things with my teacher and/or parents: ❑ Yes ❑ No

Do You Want To Meet With Your Counselor?
Why Would You & How Could You?

Know When You Need to See Your Counselor: Do you ever feel overwhelmed by everything going on in your life? Maybe you sometimes don't feel in control of your emotions. You might be angry, sad, or find yourself worried all the time. These are all good reasons to visit with your counselor and talk about your feelings.

Feel Free to Talk to Your Counselor: Sometimes it's hard when you need help. You might feel embarrassed about talking to someone, but that's what your counselor is there for!

Understand That Counselors Want to Help You: Sometimes you might talk to the counselor even if you didn't request an appointment. Remember, when you see the counselor, you are NOT in trouble. Your counselor is just checking in to see how things are going.

Decide What's on Your Mind: Before you go, think about what you want to talk about. Maybe you are having trouble with school. Maybe you are worried about something that has happened with friends and family. Thinking about what you want to talk about will help you organize your thoughts.

Really Listen: One thing your counselor does when you meet together is help you come up with a possible solution. You will brainstorm together and figure out several ideas for solving your problem. The solution only works if you really listen and then make a commitment to follow through with changes.

Be Open and Honest: Being open is a little bit different from being honest. When you are being open, it means saying what's on your mind. Being honest is telling the truth. The more honest you are, the easier it'll be to get to the bottom of a problem. If you don't tell the school counselor what's really bothering you, they can't help.

How Can You Make an Appointment? At our school, you can make an appointment to see the counselor by_____

_____

Counselor "Check–In" Passes

Counselors: Cut these passes out for the students to keep in their academic advisement folder. If they want to come see you for an additional academic advisement "check-in", this is how they can do this.

Date _____

Name _____

Teacher _____

I want to:

❑ Show you some work that I am proud of.

❑ Talk about a problem I'm having with my work.

❑ Discuss a problem that is on my mind.

Date _____

Name _____

Teacher _____

I want to:

❑ Show you some work that I am proud of.

❑ Talk about a problem I'm having with my work.

❑ Discuss a problem that is on my mind.

Date _____

Name _____

Teacher _____

I want to:

❑ Show you some work that I am proud of.

❑ Talk about a problem I'm having with my work.

❑ Discuss a problem that is on my mind.

Date _____

Name _____

Teacher _____

I want to:

❑ Show you some work that I am proud of.

❑ Talk about a problem I'm having with my work.

❑ Discuss a problem that is on my mind.

What Goal Would Be Appropriate for This Student?

The following students in your class are in academic advisement. We will be tracking specific goals for them. Please let me know a goal that you would like them to work on.

Student Name	Goal

Some ideas of goals would be:

A. Student will complete his/her class work.

B. Student will turn in homework on time.

C. Student will improve in knowing times tables.

D. Student will arrive to school on time.

Please try to be specific on the goal. Each week, you will be letting me know 1-10 (10 being great progress, and 1 being needs great improvement), how the student is doing on this goal. Make sure the goal you write down will be easy for you to rate 1-10. Thanks!

Weekly Goal Tracker

Date_____   Week # _____

10   *Great progress!*

9

8

7

6

5

4

3

2

1   *Really need to improve! You can do better!*

_____'s

goal is _____

_____

_____

Teachers: Please rate him/her 1-10 on how he/she did on this goal this week.

Comments:_____

_____

_____

(Teacher: return this to_____)

Students:

Your teacher rated you a _____ out of 10.

What helped/prevented you with your goal?

_____

_____

_____

_____

Are you on the right track ? ☐ Yes ☐ No

Parent Signature_____

Parent Comments: _____

_____

_____

Individual Goal Graphing Sheet

Student Name_____   Year/Semester_____

	session 1	session 2	session 3	session 4	session 5	session 6	session 7	session 8		
10										
9										
8										
7										
6										
5										
4										
3										
2										
1										

In session _____My goal is _____

In session _____My goal is _____

In session _____My goal is _____

(Please note that sometimes a goal might change, so space above is provided to list subsequent goals)

Keeping Track of the Groups Points

Goal Points: Goal points can be earned by students according to what degree they achieve their goal. If a teacher gives a student 8 out of 10 on their weekly goal then the counselor will mark 8 in the goal points column for that session.

Extra Points: Extra points can be earned by students in a variety of different ways. The counselor can give extra points if students are punctual, responsible, or have insightful answers. These points are up to the counselor's discretion.

An idea to reinforce success on earning points is to allow the student with the most points after every 3 (or so) sessions to choose their favorite candy which will be provided to the group the next session.

Student Name	Session ___		Session ___		Session ___		Session ___		Session ___		Session ___		Session ___		Session ___		TOTAL
	Goal Points	Extra Points	Goal Points	Extra Points	Goal Points	Extra Points	Goal Points	Extra Points	Goal Points	Extra Points	Goal Points	Extra Points	Goal Points	Extra Points	Goal Points	Extra Points	

Individual Session
Appointment Cards

Your Individual
Academic
Advisement
Appointment is: _____

Day: _____

Time: _____

Location: _____

Please bring: _____

_____

Your Individual
Academic
Advisement
Appointment is: _____

Day: _____

Time: _____

Location: _____

Please bring: _____

_____

Your Individual
Academic
Advisement
Appointment is: _____

Day: _____

Time: _____

Location: _____

Please bring: _____

_____

Your Individual
Academic
Advisement
Appointment is: _____

Day: _____

Time: _____

Location: _____

Please bring: _____

_____

Group Session
Appointment Cards

Your Individual
Academic
Advisement
Appointment is: _____

Day: _____

Time: _____

Location: _____

Please bring: _____

_____

Your Individual
Academic
Advisement
Appointment is: _____

Day: _____

Time: _____

Location: _____

Please bring: _____

_____

Your Individual
Academic
Advisement
Appointment is: _____

Day: _____

Time: _____

Location: _____

Please bring: _____

_____

Your Individual
Academic
Advisement
Appointment is: _____

Day: _____

Time: _____

Location: _____

Please bring: _____

_____

Suggestions for
Closure of Session

Here are some ideas of how to close this session.

YOU CAN DISCUSS WITH THE STUDENTS:

A plan for working on their goal

When the next meeting will be

Any forms that need to be returned

What topics will be discussed at the next meeting

Answer any questions the student has

Address any concern the student might have

Chapter 3:
Icebreakers

Overview:
Icebreakers should be the opening part of each group session of academic advisement.

Within each lesson plan for the icebreakers you will see:

Materials: This will tell you what extraneous materials you will need for this icebreaker.

Time needed: This gives you an approximation of how long the activity might last.

Procedures: This tells you a step-by-step outline of how to implement the activity.

Icebreaker Format

For each group session, an icebreaker should be done to start the group. Why? Icebreakers are done as a warm up activity to ease tension, facilitate group bonding, and as a ritual to start the group session. There are ten icebreakers to choose from in Chapter 3. The counselor can choose any of these icebreakers (or use one of their own) to start each group session.

Contents

MIND BOGGLERS

CYCLE CYCLE CYCLE	**BA** **BY**
NANA SALAD	A L I G 8 R
$\dfrac{\text{MAN}}{\text{BOARD}}$	N W O D
L K YOU O O	GROUND FEET FEET FEET FEET FEET FEET

From Bowman. (2003). *201 Amazing Mind Bogglers That Can Be Used to Teach Kids Critical lessons About Learning & Life*. Chapin: SC. YouthLight, Inc., www.youthlightbooks.com

Riddles are Brain Food!

Materials: Riddles (see below)

Time needed: 5-8 minutes

Procedures:

1. Ask the students, "What should a runner do before a race?" (answer: prepare, warm up or stretch out)

2. Discuss how we will now warm up our brains so that our brains are ready for a good work out.

3. Tell the students, "I will now ask you some riddles/brainteasers, and if you can come up with the answer raise your hand."

   Riddles:

   What gets wetter and wetter the more it dries? A TOWEL

   What can you catch but not throw? A COLD

   I can run but not walk. What am I? NOSE

   What's black and white and red all over?
   SUNBURNED SKUNK, NEWSPAPER, EMBARRASSED ZEBRA

   What goes around the world but stays in a corner? A STAMP

4. Challenge the students to find a riddle at home from parents, siblings, or the internet and share it with the group next time.

(The above riddles were gathered from <u>various sources.</u>
<u>More riddles are available on many internet sites.</u>)

How Many Words Can You Find?

Materials: Worksheet, page 38

Time needed: 5-10 minutes

Procedures:
1. Tell the group, "This activity is intended to serve as a warm-up exercise for the brain." (This works well when you are doing activities about learning styles).

2. Explain that the leader will write a word on the board that contains at least 7 letters. The object of this game is to see how many smaller (2-letter, 3-letter, etc.) words the students can make using the letters in the leader's word.

3. **Example:** If the leader's word is - **BOWLING.**

   2-letter words:
   in.....on.....no.....go

   3-letter words
   bow....low....owl....oil...

   4-letter words
   glow....boil....bowl...

4. Distribute page 38 for the students to use. In the 3 minutes you allow them, have them find as many words as they can.

5. At the end of the three minutes, the leader can give one point to students for each legitimate word found. (Stress the importance of warming up the brain and try to de-emphasize "winning.")

How Many Words Can You Find?

2 LETTER WORDS	3 LETTER WORDS

4 LETTER WORDS	5 (OR MORE) LETTER WORDS

Last Letter Game

Materials: None

Time needed: 3-5 minutes

Procedures:

1. Ask the entire group to sit in a circle.

2. The leader chooses a word (example: class). The first student must then take the LAST letter in the leader's word (S) and give a word starting with the letter S (example: special) The next student then takes the LAST letter of the previous word (L) and gives a word starting with that letter.

3. Example of evolution of the game: Class, special, lost, tree, everything, goal, letter, round....

    Variations: Use a timer to see how quickly they can go around the circle.

Class... Special... Lost... Tree... Everything... Goal... Letter... Round...

Rescue Ship: A Cooperative Game

Materials: 3-8 hula-hoops, and signs pages (41-42)

Time needed: 15 minutes (if you choose this activity your group session should be extended to 45 minutes)

Procedures:

1. Prior to the activity place the Titanic sign on the following page in one designated area of the room and rescue ship sign (page 42) in another area.

2. Explain to students, "You are passengers on the Titanic. Suddenly the ship has hit an iceberg and is sinking. The object of the game is for all the students to escape from the Titanic to the rescue ship, using the lifeboats (hula hoops) to cross the freezing water. The only way to cross the water is to be inside a lifeboat. When there is someone inside a lifeboat, it cannot be moved. Students are not allowed to touch the water outside of the lifeboats and if anyone does, he/she is sent back to the Titanic to start over again."

3. Allow students to have the opportunity to discover how to travel from the Titanic to the rescue ship without the leader's help.

   Although students should problem-solve to find a solution, here is one potential solution they might come up with: Students can use the lifeboats in a rotating fashion, therefore needing a minimum of 2 lifeboats to travel. To travel, an empty lifeboat must be placed in front. Without touching the freezing water, students move forward and inside the front lifeboat. The rear lifeboat, that should now be empty, is then picked up, passed, and moved to become the new front lifeboat and the process is repeated. One enhancement might be to play "Titanic," soundtrack in the background.

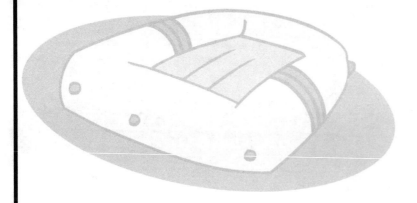

Group Juggle

Materials: 3 or 4 objects that can be thrown from person to person around a circle (ball, bean bag, etc.). It is best to have objects that are different shapes or at least different color objects to differentiate them.

Time needed: 5-8 minutes

Procedures:

1. The group stands in a circle.

2. The group leader throws a ball to another person in the circle and says their name.

3. That person throws to a person who has not received the ball and this process goes on until everyone has received the ball.

4. The leader then explains that everyone needs to remember who they threw the ball to in this past activity.

5. This next time the activity is attempted the pattern of the ball (the order in which the ball was thrown and caught should be kept the same). This time if the ball is dropped the group needs to start over.

6. The process is then repeated throwing 2 objects (the second one is thrown a few seconds after the first) to see if the pattern can be kept without the object being dropped.

7. Questions to process:

    • How did this activity make you feel?

    • How is this activity similar to life? Similar to times you are stressed?

    • What solution helped?

    • Did confidence and organization help? How is this like life?

Back to Back

Materials: None

Time needed: 5-8 minutes

Procedures:

1. Tell the students the following instructions:

   "Stand back to back with a partner. I will give you something to discuss and when I say "go" you will turn around and discuss this topic. When time is up I will say "Back to Back." At that time you need to find a new partner and stand back to back with that partner."

2. Once the students are back to back with a new partner you can ask "Who would like to share something you discussed with your last partner?"

3. After processing the topic, repeat directions to students, "When I say "go" you will turn around and discuss a new topic. When time is up I will say "Back to Back." At that time you need to find a new partner and stand back to back with that partner."

> ### *Ideas of questions to discuss with partners:*
>
> - **What is the one thing about school that frustrates you the most?**
>
> - **What is your best memory from kindergarten or first grade?**
>
> - **Who is your favorite teacher and why?**
>
> - **How important is popularity to kids in your class?**

Over Here, Over Here

This activity works best in a group with a minimum of 9 students

Materials: none

Time needed: 5 minutes

Procedures:

1. Ask students to get into groups of 3 or 4 and face each other in a circle.

2. Tell students to figure out within the group who is the tallest.

3. Tell them, "Now, the tallest student needs to step out of the circle and on the count of three the group will tell that student, 'See ya!'"

4. In order for that student to find a new group, the members need to invite a new student to the empty space in their group by yelling, "Over here! Over here!" This forms a new group.

5. When all new groups are formed, the leader will ask the groups to determine which child in the group has the most people living in his/her house.

6. The counselor will ask that in each group that student needs to step out of their circle and on the count of three the group will tell that student, "See ya!"

7. In order for that student to find a new group, the members need to invite a student to the empty space in their group by yelling, "Over here! Over here!"

8. This process can be repeated with other questions (who is the oldest, newest to the school, etc.)

QUESTIONS TO PROCESS:

- *How did it feel to be sent away from the group?*
- *How did it feel when you were invited to the new group?*
- *How does being left out affect kids at school?*
- *How can inviting a student into a group or activity help them at school?*

A Brain Maze Leaves Me in a Haze

Materials: Worksheet, page 47

Time needed: 5 minutes

Procedures:

1. Distribute the worksheet to the students.

2. Tell students that this maze will be a contest.

3. Once the students have started, tell them they have one minute to finish this.

4. After one minute is up, tell them to put their pencils down regardless if anyone has finished the maze.

QUESTIONS TO DISCUSS :

- *How did the time restraint effect your concentration?*

- *Do time limits make you stressed?*

- *Did your attitude change when you were stressed?*

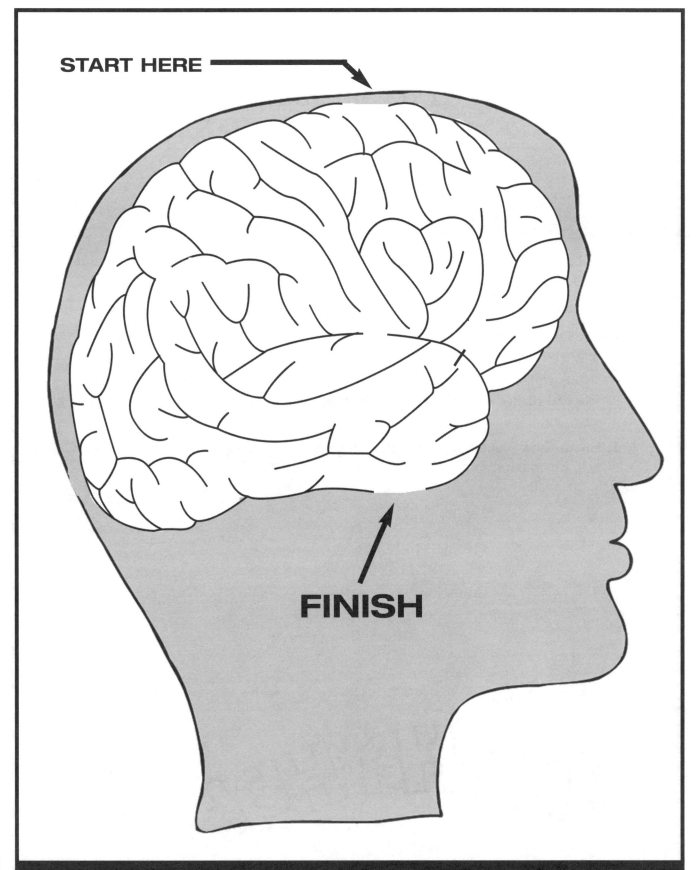

A Brain Maze Leaves Me in a Haze

Do your Brain and Body Cooperate?

Materials: None

Time needed: 3-5 minutes

1. Tell the students that we will begin today's lesson by exercising our brain and our bodies.

2. Tell the students,

   "Everyone needs to sit in a chair. While sitting in the chair, lift your right foot off the floor and make clockwise circles."

   "Now, while doing this, draw the number "6" in the air with your right hand. Your foot will change directions." (It's truly impossible to continue your leg circling clockwise, and it will cause some good laughs.)

3. Discuss how some things are difficult for the brain to do and that laughter can usually help frustrations.

Chapter 4:
Individual Session One

Overview:

After the counselor has met with the advisement group twice, it is time to meet with each student individually to discuss academic progress and concerns. Individual sessions should last about 15 minutes. In this session, several things should be covered (see the agenda page 51). The students should have a clear idea about his/her goals and progress by session's end.

Time needed for each individual session: 15-20 minute session

Before this session what does the counselor need to do?
- Get weekly goal tracker from teacher (page 26)
- Send appointment card to students (page 29-30)
- Make copies of parent permission/questionnaire to send home (page 54 or 55)

Contents

Sample Memo to Teachers

Teachers,

In the next couple of days, you will see appointment cards in your boxes for the students who are participating in academic advisement. They will be meeting individually with me for 15 minutes to discuss their progress. In order for me to have an idea of how the student is doing I'm requesting that you fill out this "weekly goal rating" sheet. In turn, I will be sending you progress notes so that you know how your student is doing. I hope this program will serve as a great strategy, a way to help the student, and a support to you in your efforts to help these kids succeed!

Thanks!

School Counselor

Note to counselor: Weekly goal rating sheet is on page 26 Progress notes are on page 56.

Scheduling Issues

There are several issues that might come up in scheduling individual appointments. If a particular student is not punctual, a possible solution is to schedule that student directly after a more responsible student. This student can help find the chronically tardy student to ensure he/she makes the appointment.

Agenda for 1st Individual Session

- Welcome student
- Counselor can reinforce punctuality with an "extra point"
- Student should complete worksheet (page 53) "How Do You Feel About …?"
- Send home parent questionnaire (page 54 or 55)
- Discuss progress notes from teacher (page 56)
- Learning Styles Lesson (page 57)
- Discuss progress of the learning goal and points earned (page 28)

How Do You Feel About...?

Materials: Worksheet, page 53

Procedures:

1. Distribute worksheet on page 53 to the student.
2. The counselor goes over the following directions verbally:

"This is an activity for me to get to know you a little better. There are no right or wrong answers. Circle the number that describes how you feel about the topic listed to the right. 10 is a score that means you have very positive feelings about it and 1 means you feel negatively."

How Do You Feel About...?

Name _____   Date _____

Please rate the following items 1-10.

Homework   1 --- 2 --- 3 --- 4 --- 5 --- 6 --- 7 --- 8 --- 9 --- 10
☹   ☺

Reading   1 --- 2 --- 3 --- 4 --- 5 --- 6 --- 7 --- 8 --- 9 --- 10
☹   ☺

Recess   1 --- 2 --- 3 --- 4 --- 5 --- 6 ---7 ---- 8 --- 9 ---10
☹   ☺

Math   1 --- 2 --- 3 --- 4 --- 5 --- 6 ---7 ---- 8 --- 9 ---10
☹   ☺

Your Family   1 --- 2 --- 3 --- 4 --- 5 --- 6 ---7 ---- 8 --- 9 ---10
☹   ☺

Classwork   1 --- 2 --- 3 --- 4 --- 5 --- 6 ---7 ---- 8 --- 9 ---10
☹   ☺

Friends   1 --- 2 --- 3 --- 4 --- 5 --- 6 ---7 ---- 8 --- 9 ---10
☹   ☺

Writing   1 --- 2 --- 3 --- 4 --- 5 --- 6 ---7 ---- 8 --- 9 ---10
☹   ☺

Your Teacher   1 --- 2 --- 3 --- 4 --- 5 --- 6 ---7 ---- 8 --- 9 ---10
☹   ☺

Sports   1 --- 2 --- 3 --- 4 --- 5 --- 6 ---7 ---- 8 --- 9 ---10
☹   ☺

Academic Advisement

Name of Student _____

As you know, your child is participating in an Academic Advisement Program. This letter is to let you know I have recently met with your child and would like the opportunity to get some information from you. Please let me know if you have any questions and feel free to reach me at _____. Thanks!

What is your major concern with your child's academics? _____

_____

_____

Please check which of the following issue(s) contribute(s) to your child's academic difficulties:

❏ Social/Emotional Issues   ❏ Attention Issues/ Distractibility
❏ Behavior   ❏ Motivation
❏ Test-Taking Skills   ❏ Work Completion
❏ Homework   ❏ Other: _____

What things do you do at home to support your child's academics?

_____

_____

_____

_____

Please return to your child's counselor by _____.

Thank you for your support,

School Counselor

Phone #: _____

QUESTIONARIO DEL PADRE PARA

EL PROGRAMA DE CONSEJO ACADEMICO

Nombre del estudiante:_____

      Como sabe, su hijo esta participando en un programa de consejo académico. Esta carta es para avisarle que recienmente me he reunido con su hijo y me gustária la oportunidad de obtener información de usted. Déjeme saber si tiene alguna pregunta. Me puede llamar a (___) _____. Gracias.

¿Cual es la major preocupacion con los problemas academicos de su hijo?

Marque cuales de los puntos siguentes que contribuyen a las dificultades academicas de su hijo:

__ Cosas sociales o emotivas

__ Atención/distracción

__ Comportamiento

__ Motivación

__ Habilidad de tomar examenes

__ Cumpliendo tarea o trabajos

__ Tarea

__ Otro punto:

¿ Cuales cosas hace en la casa para apoyar los estudios de su hijo?

Porfavor devuielva este papel al consejor de su hijo para _____ fecha. Gracias por su apoyo.

Consejor de escuela_____

Telefono_____

PROGRESS NOTES
From Counselor to Teacher

Counselors: You can fill these forms out to keep teachers informed about the student's progress in Academic Advisement.

To:_____ From: Counselor

Date: _____

I wanted to keep you informed about how _____ is doing.

For this session, did the student:

❑ bring what he/she was supposed to?
❑ come on time?
❑ take responsibility for actions in group?

His/her goal progress:_____

_____

Comments/Topics discussed: _____

_____

_____

To:_____ From: Counselor

Date: _____

I wanted to keep you informed about how _____ is doing.

For this session, did the student:

❑ bring what he/she was supposed to?
❑ come on time?
❑ take responsibility for actions in group?

His/her goal progress:_____

_____

Comments/Topics discussed: _____

_____

_____

Learning Styles

Materials: Worksheet, page 58

Procedures:

1. Distribute page 58, 'The Learning Styles Inventory.'
2. Students should follow the directions listed on the sheet:

   Directions:
   1. Fold the paper on the vertical line that says "fold here."
   2. Put a check in the column next to the sentences that describe you.
   3. Unfold the paper and circle the x on the same line of your check marks.
   4. Next, add up the number of circled x's in each column and mark the totals.

The Learning Styles Inventory

Name _____   Date _____

Directions:

1. Fold the paper lengthwise down the dotted line. Check the boxes beside the sentences that describe you.

	auditory	visual	kinesthetic
☐ I remember something better if I write it down.		X	
☐ I need to take a lot of study breaks.			X
☐ Writing is difficult for me.	X		
☐ If there is music or noise around, I can't concentrate.		X	
☐ I learn well by using math cubes, counters and acting things out.			X
☐ I like to hear directions told to me rather than reading them.	X		
☐ I hum or talk to myself when I am bored	X		
☐ To remember something better, I get a picture of it in my head.		X	
☐ I use my hands when I am talking.			X
☐ I learn well by reading things out loud.	X		
☐ I like to see what I am learning better than hearing it explained.		X	
☐ I like to do things myself to really understand things.			X
TOTAL			

2. Unfold the paper and circle the x on the same line of your check marks.
3. Next, add up the number of circled x's in each column and mark the totals.

What type of learner are you?

☐ auditory   ☐ visual   ☐ kinesthetic

From King, L. (2005). *Making the link: Helping students link school habits with the world of work.*
Chapin: SC. YouthLight, Inc

Monitoring Progress

Counselors: Below are some discussion points you can go over with the students.

LEARNING GOAL

What is your learning goal and were you successful in accomplishing your goal this week?

How was your learning goal success this week?

Are you pleased with your progress at working towards your goal?

If so, how?

Have you been doing so well at your goal that we should choose another goal?

POINTS

Did you earn any extra points this week in Academic Advisement?

Why or why not?

How could you improve/maintain your classroom behavior as if you were always earning extra points?

TEACHER NOTES

Have you read your teacher's comments about your goal?

What is your reaction to this feedback?

Chapter 5:
Small Group Content
and Lesson Plans

Overview:

The academic advisement group sessions should always start with an icebreaker and have a skill-building activity. The closure activity can be a closing circle reviewing how everyone did on the weekly goal. The skill-building content is flexible according to the needs of the group. (See Needs Assessment page 63).

The outline below describes what types of lesson plans are included in this chapter, which can be used for the group sessions. Of course these lessons can be adapted for use in individual sessions as needed.

Contents

Which Lessons Should Be Included in Group?

Students,

Which topics do you feel are important for you to review and practice? Put a number next to the subjects according to how important you think the topic is for you to discuss.

3 = most important for me to work on

2 = somewhat important for me to work on

1 = not important for me to work on

_____Motivation (trying hard and being excited about learning)

_____Procrastination (not using time wisely)

_____Goal Setting

_____Learning Styles (how you learn)

_____Test Anxiety (being nervous about taking tests)

_____Testing Skills

_____Handling Stress and Pressure

_____Turning In Assignments

_____General Study Skills

_____Organization

Introduction to Learning Styles

Materials: Worksheet (page 58) which has been previously completed by students, page 65-66, highlighters

Procedures:

1. Ask students, "What is a learning style? What are the three learning styles?"

2. Use page 65 as a visual in teaching the three learning styles.

3. Students should review the inventory (page 58) that they filled out during the individual session.

4. Go around the group and have everyone share what learning style they most identify with. Ask students if they agree with what the inventory surmised.

5. Distribute 'Tips for Learning Styles', page 66.

6. Ask students to cut out the section on page 65 that applies to them and glue/tape these 'tips for learning' to the outside of their advisement folder.

7. Students can highlight one or two tips that they plan to use in the next week.

Explanation of Learning Styles

<u>**LEARNING STYLE**</u> refers to the process in which one understands information.

The three basic learning styles are:

Visual Learning

Learning through seeing

Auditory Learning

Learning through hearing

Kinesthetic Learning

Learning through movement or touch

Tips for your learning styles

 ***Tips for studying using your
<u>VISUAL learning style</u>***

Coordinate notebooks for each subject in a different color
Use post it notes, checklists, and reminder cards
Use pictures, charts, graphs to reinforce information

 ***Tips for studying using your
<u>AUDITORY learning style</u>***

Leave important reminders on tape recorders
Discuss daily outline of schedule and tasks out loud
Study in groups for tests
Use "Books on Tape"
Read aloud
Edit your work out loud

 ***Tips for studying using your
<u>KINESTHETIC learning style</u>***

Use computers to do written work
Play with a stress ball or silly putty while working
Place post it notes on important parts of work
Highlight main ideas

Procrastination… How to Avoid It

Materials: Worksheet pages 68-70, highlighters

Procedures:

1. Allow students to guess what the topic is going to be, by playing hangman. (The word that they are guessing is PROCRASTINATION).

2. Distribute small strips of paper to students and ask them to write down the definition of "procrastination" (even if it's just a guess).

3. The counselor then can read aloud all of the strips of paper and see if anyone is close. Then, the counselor can tell them the correct definition.

4. Allow student to give an example of a time that they procrastinated.

5. Ask students to read page 68 and highlight three interesting points.

6. Review page 69 and use page 70 as a sample.

7. Students can review the sample (page 70) with their parents and use the Task Completion Sheet (page 69) for one task they do over the next week.

I'll Do It in a Minute...
Procrastination and How to Avoid It!

What is procrastination? Procrastination means waiting until the last minute to do tasks that are supposed to get done. Are you one of those people who waits until the last minute to do things? Problems can develop when we leave tasks until the last minute. Here are tips to help prevent procrastination.

CUT DOWN A TASK INTO SMALLER PARTS — If you have a large task, it doesn't have to be done at once. Start with a small part of the task, one step at a time.

BE SPECIFIC ABOUT EACH SMALL STEP OF THE TASK — Tell yourself "I will read three pages of chapter 6 on Saturday before lunch," rather than "I need to read chapter 6 this week."

MAKE LISTS OF THINGS TO BE DONE — Check items off of your list as you complete each task. Being able to cross something off often inspires us to do another.

USE SPARE TIME – If you have fifteen minutes to wait for dinner, use your time to write notes about a paper or plan for a project. Don't expect to get it all done in one sitting.

TRY A BUDDY SYSTEM — Arrange with a friend to give each other feedback on each other's plans and progress.

DON'T TRY TO BE PERFECT — Trying your best is better than not doing it at all. For writing assignments, put something down on paper even if you aren't sure you love the ideas. You can edit your work later.

AVOID DISTRACTIONS — TV, video games, telephone calls, and music can be very distracting and only give you excuses to delay doing your work.

ADDRESS YOUR FEARS — What is preventing you from action? Are you afraid or embarrassed about doing something wrong? Talk about your fears and admit them to yourself... then get started!

Which one are you going to try? _____

When are you going to try it? _____

Task Completion Sheet

(or in other words… how to avoid procrastination)

What is the task? _____

Divide the task into at least three smaller parts.

a. _____

b. _____

c. _____

Schedule when are you going to do part A?_____

Schedule when are you going to do part B?_____

Schedule when are you going to do part C?_____

Check off the following ONLY when they are completed:

❑ I did part A.

❑ I did part B.

❑ I did part C.

Task Completion Sheet

(or in other words… how to avoid procrastination)

What is the task? <u>Read Chapter 4 (which is 15 pages) in the next two days.</u>

Divide the task into at least three smaller parts.

    a. <u>I will read the first five pages before I go to bed.</u>

    b. <u>Tomorrow I will read the next five pages.</u>

    c. <u>The day after tomorrow I will read the last pages.</u>

Schedule when are you going to do part A? <u>Today before I go to bed.</u>

Schedule when are you going to do part B? <u>Tomorrow</u>

Schedule when are you going to do part C? <u>The day after tomorrow.</u>

Check off the following ONLY when they are completed:

☑ I did part A.

☑ I did part B.

☑ I did part C.

SAMPLE

Stress Management

Are you stressed out? What does that mean?

Materials: Worksheet, page 72-73

Procedures:

1. Ask the students to brainstorm words associated with the word "stress."

2. Next, distribute and have students fill out the Stress Survey (page 72). Have them add up their totals.

3. Discuss with the group the results of their stress survey. Ask the students if they agree with these results.

4. On the back of their worksheets, have the students write four ways they relieve stress.

5. For homework, have students take home page 73, "Student Reading on Stress." Encourage students to read this with their parents or guardians and have parents sign the bottom.

Stress Survey

How do you handle stress? Rate how you typically react in each of the situations listed below. There are no right or wrong answers, only honest answers.

4 = Always   3 = Frequently   2 = Sometimes   1 = Never

Enter a number on the line before each question. When you complete the questionnaire, add up the total number of points and write it below.

_____ Do you get very angry or upset?

_____ Do you become impatient when someone interrupts your conversation?

_____ Do you have to win at games to have fun?

_____ Is it hard for you to ask for help with a problem?

_____ Do you get annoyed with the way others do their work?

_____ Do you have the habit of looking at your watch or clock often?

_____ Do you strive to always be the best at the things you do?

_____ Do you have a habit of talking quickly?

_____ Do you consider yourself hard working?

_____ Do your friends or family consider you hard working?

_____ TOTAL

On the back of this worksheet, write four ways you relieve stress.

Answer Key
If your score is between 10 and 19, chances are you might be so relaxed, that you might not be noticing the situations that are really going on around you!
A score between 20 and 28 means you have a good balance in your ability to handle and control stress.
If your score ranges between 29 and 32, your stress level is on the verge of being too tense.
If your total number of points exceeds 33 you might be stressed out to the max! You need to get help in understanding how to manage stress!

Student Reading on Stress

Directions: Read this article and answer the questions.

WHAT IS STRESS?

Stress is similar to worrying. Anything that causes a change in your life can cause stress to your body and it's important to be aware of it. Both good and bad changes are stressful. If you break your leg, the experience will be stressful. If your family wins the lottery and moves to a huge mansion, the move will still create stress.

When you have a lot of stress in your life, it can have effects that last a long time. It is like throwing a rock into a pond. After the initial splash, you experience ripples of stress. It is important to acknowledge the stress in your life when it is occurring so that you can do something to release this stress. Some people like to relax in a quiet place to rid their bodies and minds of stress. Other people like to be active and exercise to release the stress or tension. Still others like to talk to people they trust about the stress and this is also helpful. Everyone handles stress differently and it is important to know what helps you.

What is stress?_____

_____

What can cause stress? _____

_____

What do you do to relax when you are stressed? _____

_____

Did you read this and discuss this with the adults in your house? ☐ Yes ☐ No

If so, have them sign here. _____

Stress Management II
What could be stressing you out?

Materials: Worksheet, page 75

Procedures:

1. Ask students "What things in life can cause stress?" Ask students to think about times of the year that are more stressful than others.

2. Introduce the ideas that certain factors can cause stress and we call these "stress triggers."

3. Distribute page 75 and have students circle the factors that are present in their lives.

4. Have students add up the total of all the numbers that they circled.

5. Discuss results according to page 76.

What Stresses You?

Look at the list below. Circle the numeric value in the second column next to any event that has occurred in your life in the last few months.

EVENT	VALUE
DEATH OF PARENT	100
PARENTS DIVORCE	65
PUBERTY	65
DEATH OF PET	50
SERIOUS PERSONAL INJURY OR ILLNESS	45
TROUBLE AT SCHOOL	40
SERIOUS HEALTH PROBLEM OF A FAMILY MEMBER	40
GAIN OF NEW FAMILY MEMBER (new baby born or parent remarries or adopts)	35
CHANGE IN NUMBER OF ARGUMENTS WITH FAMILY OR FRIENDS	30
SLEEP LESS THAN 8 HOURS PER NIGHT	25
GETTING ATTENTION FOR PERSONAL ACHIEVEMENT (awards, grades, etc.)	25
BEGIN OR END OF SCHOOL YEAR	20
FEEL AS IF YOU HAVE NO FRIENDS	20
CHANGE IN LIVING CONDITIONS (visitors in the home, remodeling house, change in roommates)	20
SEVERE ALLERGIES	20
STANDARDIZED TESTING	15
CHANGE TO A NEW SCHOOL	15
VACATION	10
WINTER HOLIDAY SEASON	10
BIG PROJECT COMING UP	10
FEEL PRESSURE FROM AFTER SCHOOL ACTIVITY/SPORT	5

TOTAL SCORE _____

WORKSHEET

Overstressed?

How did you score? _____

How do you think this compares to others in your group? _____

_____

_____

_____

Things in your life might be making you OVERSTRESSED. Being very OVERSTRESSED over a long period of time can make you sick. Carrying a heavy stress load is like running your car engine until it runs out of gas. Sooner or later, something will break or melt down. Here are the common PHYSICAL REACTIONS to stress:

Brain: Fatigue, aches and pains, frequently crying, depression, anxiety attacks, trouble sleeping.

Gastrointestinal Tract: Ulcer, cramps and diarrhea.

Cardiovascular: High blood pressure, heart attack, abnormal heart beat, stroke.

Skin: Itchy skin rashes.

Immune System: Decreased resistance to infections.

Study-Skills
Research and Poster Making Session 1

Materials: Computers with internet capability, poster board, markers

Procedures:

1. In preparation for this session, the counselor should bookmark any websites that students might use.

2. The students should be divided into groups of 3 students. Within each group, the counselor appoints: a scribe, a computer specialist and a graphic designer. The scribe will take notes and a computer specialist will control the computer. The graphic designer will have leadership in designing the poster.

3. The counselor will assign each group one of the following topics:

    - **Ways to Organize Study Area at School and at Home**
    - **Good Note-Taking Skills**
    - **Studying for Tests**
    - **Time Management**
    - **Procrastination**
    - **Listening Skills**
    - **Test Anxiety**
    - **Learning Styles**

4. Distribute page 78 to each group.

5. Once computers are up and running, the computer specialist will access the internet sites on the assigned topic and the group can look on as the scribe takes notes.

6. At the end of the session, the counselor will retain the worksheets that the group gathered so that groups will be ready for session 2. (see page 79)

Study Wise Poster Outline

Session 1

Topic_____

Who is the Scribe?_____

Who is the Computer Specialist? _____

Who is the Graphic Designer? _____

Computer Specialist: What websites did you use? (At least 2)

_____

_____

Scribe: What are some facts that are important to include in this poster?

_____

_____

_____

Graphic Designer: What are some ideas you have for designing the poster?

_____

_____

_____

Study Wise Posters

Session 2

This is session 2 out of 2. Please refer to page 77 for session 1.

Materials: Computers with internet capability, poster board, markers

Procedures:

1. Check in with the group to make sure that they are ready to create a poster on the topic assigned to their group in the last session. (Counselor will return page 78 completed by each group last session)

2. Allow the groups to brainstorm how they will design their poster which should be completed at the end of this session.

3. Groups can present their posters and give a brief oral explanation of the study skills that were learned.

4. Posters can be displayed in the hallways to exhibit the students' work on healthy study habits.

Study Skills Newsletter

Materials: Computers with word processing software, children's books about school success skills, paper and pencil

Procedures:

1. Explain to the group that we will be creating a "Study Skills Newsletter."

2. Distribute page 81 to students.

3. Allow students to work in pairs or alone.

4. The counselor goes over page 81.

QUESTIONS TO CONSIDER:

- *What is a good name for our newsletter?*
- *What part of the newsletter do the students want to focus on?*
- *How are you going to do your job as a reporter?*
- *Do you need any materials in order to do your assignment?*

---

5. Students work on their assignments.

6. If the software is not available, counselor can print out articles that the students write and compile into a newsletter.

Newsletter Preparation Sheet

Reporter Name(s)_____

What are some ideas for names of our newsletter?
(Success Daily News, Study Skills Times, etc.)

_____

_____

_____

_____

Assignment for the newsletter:

❑ Do you want to interview someone? On what topic?_____

❑ Do you want to do research on a study skill?

❑ Do you want to review a children's book on study skills?

❑ Do you want to write a paragraph about why you do or don't like school?

What are some materials you might need to complete an article?

_____

_____

_____

_____

_____

Turning in Assignments

Materials: Worksheet, page 83, signs on construction paper that say:

Always, Sometimes, Never

Procedures:

1. Counselor should put the three signs: "Always," "Sometimes," "Never" in three separate areas around the room.

2. Ask the students to travel to the sign that would be their best response for the following statements:

ALWAYS — SOMETIMES — NEVER

- *I know what I should be doing for homework assignments.*
- *I do my homework at home.*
- *I remember to bring my homework from home to school.*
- *I turn my homework in on time.*
- *I finish my class work.*

---

3. How is homework different from classwork?

4. Distribute page 83 and go over this visual flowchart of what happens to an assignment once it is assigned.

5. Discuss the effect of what a zero does to a class grade.

What Happens When You Get an Assignment?

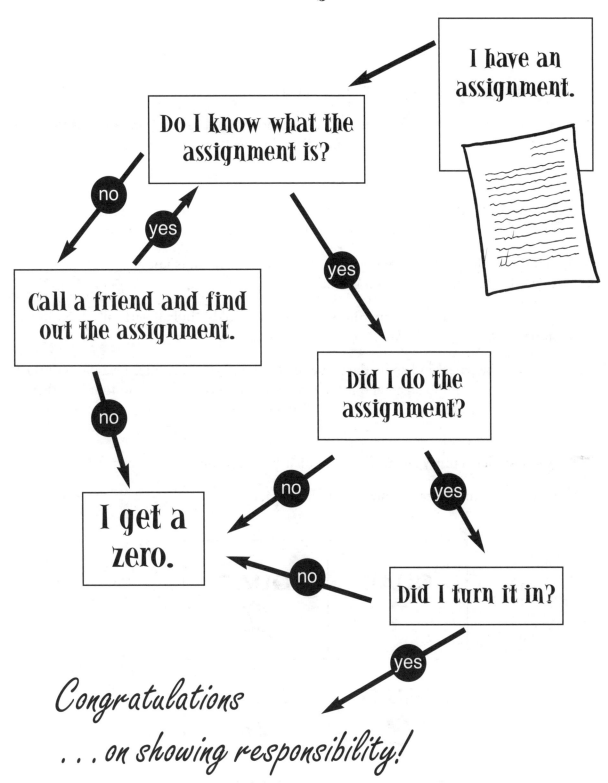

I have an assignment.

Do I know what the assignment is?

no → Call a friend and find out the assignment.

yes ↑

yes → Did I do the assignment?

Call a friend and find out the assignment. **no** → I get a zero.

Did I do the assignment? **no** → I get a zero.

yes → Did I turn it in?

Did I turn it in? **no** → I get a zero.

yes →

Congratulations ...on showing responsibility!

Organization

Materials: Worksheet, page 95 (2 copies for each student)

Procedures:

1. Distribute one copy of page 85 to the students.

2. Tell the students that they will have 15 seconds to find as many numbers as they can in consecutive order. They must find #1 and circle it then find #2 and circle it, etc.

3. After 15 seconds have passed, tell them to put their pencils down.

4. Ask which student got to the highest number. Ask this student how they accomplished the task. Ask if they had a "method to their madness" or an organized plan?

5. Tell the students that there is a trick. The key to this task is knowing that the best way to do things is usually in an organized way.

6. Have students fold their paper into 4 quadrants (Fold it in half vertically, then in half horizontally).

7. Re-open the paper and show the students that there is an organized way to find the numbers. The numbers ascend from quadrant one to two to three to four and then back to one again (so the number 1 and then 5 will be found somewhere in quadrant one.)

8. Allow students to try again when you distribute a second copy of page 85.

9. Discuss how organization helps us to be efficient.

QUAD 1	QUAD 2
QUAD 3	QUAD 4

Organization

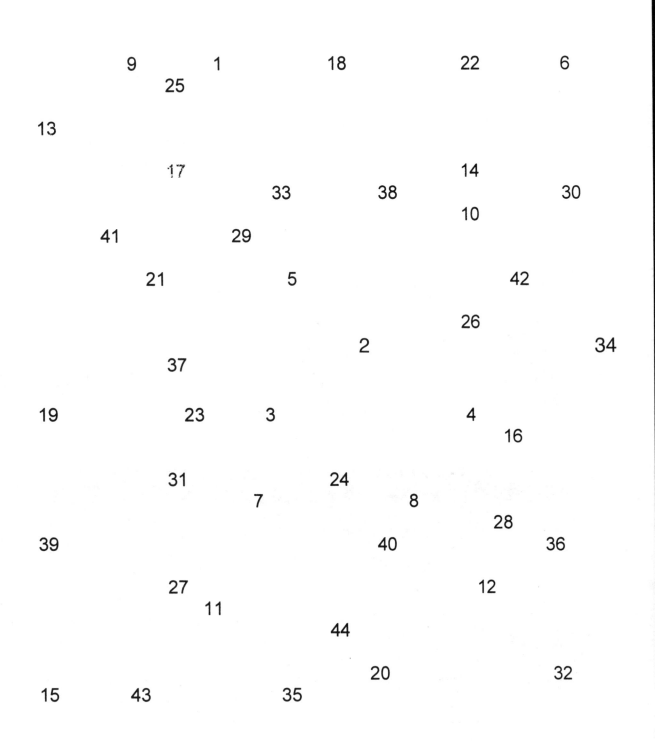

9　　　1　　　　18　　　　22　　　　6

25

13

17　　　　14

33　　　38　　　　　30

10

41　　　29

21　　　　5　　　　　42

26

2　　　　　　34

37

19　　　23　　　3　　　　4

16

31　　　24

7　　　　8

28

39　　　　　40　　　36

27　　　　　12

11

44

20　　　　32

15　　43　　　　35

Motivation

This lesson is more effective after the motivation article has been read in an individual session (See page 96)

Materials: Article on motivation (page 96), worksheet on page 87, M&M's®, mini candy bars or lollipops, small clear cups for candy, jenga® game (or just blocks you can stack).

Procedures:

1. Distribute cups to students. Explain that today for all positive behaviors they will be rewarded with an M&M®.

2. Counselor will start to reward students for ANY good behavior, good answer, or appropriate action with an M&M®.

3. Counselor will explain the following activity (all the time giving out M&M's). The object of the game is to build a tower as high as possible as a team. For each block placed on the tower you have to:

   • Say something you do or don't like about school, or
   • Say something you need help with in school.

4. As the game progresses, the counselor can increase the reward to a lollipop or mini candy bars.

5. The counselor can distribute page 87.

Discuss the following questions:

• *How did the candy motivate you?*

• *Did your motivation depend on the type of candy?*

• *Were you motivated by how much others were earning?*

• *Does competition often motivate you?*

• *What is the difference between intrinsic and extrinsic motivation? (see article pg. 87)*

Worksheet Motivation:
What Motivates You?

Directions: Put a check in the circle next to the items that help motivate you. In other words, would you work harder if it meant working towards these things as rewards?

Extrinsic Motivators

◯ **Candy**

What is your favorite candy? _____

◯ **Video Games**

◯ **Fast Food Restaurants**

What is your favorite food? _____

◯ **Teacher Complimenting You**

◯ **Not Losing Recess**

◯ **Money**

Intrinsic Motivators

◯ **Feeling Successful**

◯ **Learning**

◯ **Being Independent**

◯ **Understanding Information**

Goal Setting

Materials: A trash can (or a bucket or tub), 4 balled up pieces of paper (or tennis balls), ladder worksheet (page 90), goal cards (page 89)

Procedures:

1. Have the group separated into two teams.

2. Discuss how goal setting is similar to taking steps up a ladder. Discuss how having a plan helps keep things more organized and goals are easier to reach.

3. Invite one person from each team up to the front. Have each student ball up paper and stand across from the trash can. Tell the students that they are representing their teams and will try to throw the paper into the basket. Have them guess how many out of three they will get in the trash can. Tell them they can stand wherever they want to. See how many they can get in the basket.

4. At the end, review whether the students met their goals. Ask if they did this again, what goal would they set?

5. Discuss how people set goals for themselves in different ways. Did they stand close or far away?

6. Hand out a ladder worksheet to each group (page 90) and one goal from the goal cards (page 89). Have each group write the specific skills they would need to accomplish their assigned goal.

7. Have one representative from each group tell about how they would reach that goal.

From King, L. (2005). *Making the link: Helping students link school habits with the world of work.* Chapin: SC. YouthLight, Inc., www.youthlightbooks.com

Goal Cards

Your Goal
Make a Peanut Butter and Jelly Sandwich

Your Goal
Win the Spelling Bee

Your Goal
Run a Mile in a Race

Your Goal
Make a New Friend

Your Goal
Clean Your Room

Your Goal
Make a Snowman

Goal Setting Ladder

Come up with the steps you would take to achieve your goal.

Remember to start from the bottom and work your way up.

What is your goal?_____

My Goal

4 _____

3 _____

2 _____

1 _____

From King, L. (2005). *Making the link: Helping students link school habits with the world of work.*
Chapin: SC. YouthLight, Inc., www.youthlightbooks.com

Testing Skills and Test Anxiety

Materials: Post-its, binder, day planner/agenda book, worksheet page 92

Procedures:

1. Ask students what words come to mind when they think of "tests."

2. Discuss how you can have fear and excitement at the same time (for instance on a roller coaster), which sometimes happens on a test.

3. Look at page 92 and have students work in pairs to discuss and fill out this worksheet on how they intend on avoiding test stress.

4. When the group comes back together, have group members share their ideas with the group.

5. Next, the counselor should ask the group to focus on # 2 on page 92. Discuss how organization can reduce stress.

6. Have students get with a different partner and discuss

   - *How does their desk organization effect their work?*

   - *How is their room organized and how does this effect them?*

7. Bring out: back pack, post-its, binder, day planner/agenda book. Have students brainstorm how each of these items can assist with organization. (For instance, putting your binder in front of your backpack or putting your backpack near the door can help you remember these items.)

Avoiding Test Anxiety

TIPS TO AVOID TEST STRESS	HOW ARE YOU GOING TO DO THIS?
1. Maintain good sleeping habits, especially during the week of the test.	
2. Stay organized.	
3. Come to school on time.	
4. Maintain a healthy diet and exercise.	
5. Wear comfortable clothes during the test and maintain a comfortable and relaxed body posture during the test.	
6. Be aware of time given for the test.	
7. Read directions carefully.	
8. Don't compare yourself to other students while taking the test.	
9. If you get stressed, attempt to regain a calm attitude.	

Chapter 6:
Individual Session #2

Overview:

In this chapter the counselor will meet with the student to review their progress, and to discuss motivation.
There is an article on motivation that will be sent home so that parents can discuss this with their child.

Before this session what does the counselor need do?
Counselor needs to get feedback from teacher.
Make copies of "Counselor Appointment to Observe"

Before the next session what does the counselor need to do?
Send progress notes to teachers.
Set up classroom observation.

Contents

Agenda for 2nd Individual Session

1 Review teacher commentary and parent feedback.

2 Goal Tracker: Monitor learning goal

3 Discuss classroom observation that will occur.

4 Go over page 96, "Motivation: An Article for Students to Read"

Motivation:
An Article for Students to Read

PARENTS: Please read the following article with your child and answer the questions together.

What Should You Know About Motivation?

Student motivation means a student's desire to participate in the learning process. What motivates a student? Often, we think of student motivation in two categories. Outside motivation (sometimes called extrinsic motivation) is where a student wants to learn purely to get a reward or avoid a punishment. Teachers often motivate students by giving out candy, stickers, or taking away privileges, such as recess. These are extrinsic rewards. Inner (or intrinsic) motivation is when a student is motivated from within. Inner motivated students actively want to learn out of curiosity, enjoyment, or in order to achieve their goals. It is important to note that most successful people are motivated by both internal and external factors.

How Can Parents Help?

Parents can help motivate kids by being invested in their homework, and asking questions about school. Additionally, here are some specific things parents can do to help their children be motivated students:

- Communicate regularly with teachers.
- Create a place at home that is appropriate for studying. Good study areas are well-lit and quiet. Also, students do best when the television is off and the student is free from distractions.
- Set aside a specific time for homework each day.
- Be available if students have questions. Parents can support their children by looking over homework and giving suggestions, but should not do the homework for them.

Students who are not motivated to learn are less likely to succeed. It is important to recognize how healthy self-esteem helps keep a child motivated and in turn the student is ready for success.

What is motivation? _____

What ways can parents help keep kids motivated?

_____

_____

_____

Counselor Appointment to Observe

Teachers,

In the next week, I intend on coming to do a classroom observation on your

student_____. I'll be in the classroom for only

about 10-20 minutes and I'd love to observe a time when you are doing

_____. If you could give me an idea

of some good time slots to observe, I would greatly appreciate it.

Thanks,

School Counselor

Chapter 7:
Final Group Session

Overview:

In this group session, students will review how they are doing academically, and the things on which they still need to improve.

Before this session what does the counselor need do?
Make copies of parent invitation (page 103).
Calculate point totals to identify who should choose snack for "reunion" (page 120).

Contents

Final Group Agenda

1 Group Point Totals (Page 28)

2 Self-Evaluation

3 Maintenance Plan for Continued Success and Growth

4 Parent Invitation

5 Celebrate Success

Self-Evaluation

What Has Been Helpful? Questions for students to answer.

1. What was the most helpful thing about the academic advisement group?

   _____

2. What skills have you improved on in the past few weeks? _____

   _____

3. Would you recommend this program for other students? _____

   Why? _____

   _____

4. What things in school are still difficult for you? _____

   _____

5. How might you work to improve this? _____

   _____

   _____

Pledge for Continued Success and Growth

I PLEDGE THE FOLLOWING TO CONTINUE MY SCHOOL SUCCESS:

(Only check off the things that are realistic…. things that you really will do!)

❏ I will read _____ minutes a night.

❏ I will keep my desk organized.

❏ I will use the tips for my learning style,
which is _____.

❏ I will avoid procrastination.

❏ I will turn in assignments on time.

❏ I will stay motivated.

❏ I will set realistic goals.

❏ I will set a plan for how to reach my goals.

❏ I will reduce my stressful feelings by _____

_____.

WORKSHEET

to Discuss Academic Progress

Date_____

Dear Parent/Guardian,

As you know, I have been meeting with _____
in an academic advisement program. This program is coming to an end and I wanted to communicate with you a summary of your child's progress. I have had an opportunity to get to know your child better, observed in his/her classroom and have a sense of his/her work ethic. If you would like to set up a conference to discuss your child's progress, please return this form.

Thank you for your continued support,

School Counselor

- -

I would like to have a

❑ Phone Conference with the counselor

❑ Conference at school

    ❑ With my child attending

    ❑ With my child's teacher attending

Good days/time for our conference would be _____

Parent/Guardian name_____

Phone #_____Email_____

INVITACION PARA DISCUTIR EL PROGRESO ACADEMICO

Fecha: _____

Estimado Padre/Guardian

Como sabe, he estado juntandome con _____ en un programa de consejo académico. Este programa se está acabando y quiero communicarme con usted sobre el progresso de su hijo. He conocido su hijo mejor, observadolo en su sala de clase y tengo una idea de su ética de trabajo. Si quiere una conferencia para discutir el progresso de su hijo por favor devuelva esta forma.

Gracias por su apoyo.

Consejero de la escuela _____

Quisiera una

___ Conferencia telefonica con el consejero

___ Conferencia en la escuela con

__ mi hijo presente

__ el maestro de mi hijo presente

Dias buenos para nuestra conferencia serían _____

Padre/Guardian_____ _____

Teléfono _____   E-mail _____

Chapter 8:
Final Individual Session

Overview:

This session is the culminating meeting of the program. Parents can be invited to attend this session as well. This session should be a time to reflect on growth and plan for continued academic goal setting.

Before this session what does the counselor need to do?
- Make sure individual graph of goal is complete (page 27)
- Send teacher feedback form to teachers (page 108)

Contents

Agenda for Individual Session with Student

1 — *Review of what we have done in academic advisement.*

2 — *Review teacher commentary and counselor observation.*

3 — *Review growth chart of individual goal.*

4 — *Review pledge for growth (page 102).*

5 — *Discuss follow-up visits or potential group reunion*

Teacher Feedback Form

First, I would like to thank you for your support in the Academic Advisement Program. Secondly, I would like to get feedback on what you felt was helpful and what might make this program better in the future. I realize that there was some paperwork involved in this process for you and the monitoring of the students goals would not have been possible without your help. Working together on behalf of children to help them achieve is a great accomplishment. Thank you for all you do to go above and beyond for your students.

Please answer the following questions with a rating of 1-5.

1 **2** **3** **4** **5**

NOT AT ALL   NOT MUCH   ADEQUATELY   YES   VERY MUCH

_____1. Do you think this program helped to improve student academics?

_____2. Do you think students enjoyed this experience?

_____3. Do you think the weekly goal helped the students achieve?

_____4. Do you think parents were involved enough in this program?

_____5. Do you feel that you were made aware of student progress?

What other feedback would be helpful for me to know about the Academic Advisement Program?

Again, thanks for your extra efforts in helping your students!!

Chapter 9:
Words of Wisdom
from the Experts

Overview:

This chapter will have letters/articles on various topics. There are articles for parents and also age appropriate articles for students to read.

Contents

Words for Parents from a Pediatrician

My child is having academic difficulty... what should I do?

By Stephen King MD

The goal of each parent is to help their children become successful adults. The best way to accomplish this is to provide proper education, motivation and encouragement so that children will be successful students (truly their first job). Some of our children struggle with school, and it is our job as parents to guide these challenged students in a direction that will make them feel worthwhile. You should not blame yourself for your child's performance but you can reassure them and get them some help.

First and foremost in order to help them, we need to know the reasons that they are struggling. Do they have a medical problem that is undetected (10% of school problems are related to a medical illness)? To ensure no problem is going undetected, it is important to have regular checkups annually. It is imperative that you bring the school problems, to the doctor's attention. There are many physical abnormalities like diabetes, thyroid disorders, seizures, tic disorders, allergic phenomenon and other neurological problems that can affect learning. After ruling out the physical problems we can concentrate on social and communication disorders including the inability to understand social cues and non-verbal cues from the teacher or other students. There is also the possibility that your child may have a learning disability. These are important things to ask your child's teacher or doctor about if you are concerned.

Finally there is the ever present and often over diagnosed attention deficit disorder. This disorder can include behaviors where a child is impulsive, disorganized, daydreams, and cannot follow instructions. They might have difficulty following the rules of the classroom, yet they are bright and quite capable. After the physical medical problems are eliminated, you will need to get feedback from the school to your doctor so that she/he can sit down and review this information with you. You might request feedback from the teachers, counselors and psychologists at school. They or the doctor might suggest a battery of psychometric testing (IQ, achievement and inventory/checklist for attention) to complete the workup.

When all of the data is obtained, you might be directed to get help in the areas of special education, medical interventions, psychological counseling, or perhaps family counseling. All of these suggestions are for the family to ultimately decide. It is vital for the school and families to work together so that we can keep your child on the successful path to becoming a productive and happy adult.

Stephen King, MD has been a pediatrician for 25 years in the Atlanta area and often consults with parents on school related issues.

CONSEJOS DE UN PEDIATRA PARA PADRES

¿ Mi hijo esta encontrando dificultad con los estudios. Que debo de hacer?

La meta de cada padre es ayudar sus niños llegar hacer adultos con exito. La mejor manera de cumplir esto es proveer una correcta edicacion, motivacion, y amparo para que los ninos sean estudiantes prosperos (Realmente su primer ocupacion). Algunos de nuestros hijos luchan con la escuela y nuestro trabajo como padres es dirijir estos estudiantes desafiados en una dereccion que los va a hacer sentir valerosos. No debe de echarse la culpa por la accion de sus hijos pero puede darles confianza y buscarles ayuda.

Primero, y muy importante para ayudarlos tenemos que encontrar las razones porque están batallando. Tienen un problema medico (10 % de problemas con escuela estan basado en una enfermedad)? Para asegurar que no tienen problemas de salud occultos es importante que tengan un chequeo regular cada año. Es imperativo que traiga los problemas de escuela a la atencion del doctor. Hay muchas abnormalidades físicas como Diabetes, problemas de la teroid, ataques, problemas nerviosos, alergia y otros problemas neurológicos que pueden afectar erudicion. Despues de eliminar los problemas fisicos podemos concentrarnos en los problemas social y de comunicacion incluyendo la inabilidad de entender los medios sociales y no-verbales de los maestros y otros alumnus. Tambien hay la posibilidad que su hijo tenga una disabilidad aprendiendo. Estas son cosas importantes preguntarle al maestro o al doctor de su hijo si esta preocupado.

En final, hay el siempre presente, y muchas veces mal usado diagnostico de Dificiencia de Atencion (Attention Deficit Disorder). Este disorden puede incluier modos de acciones donde un nino es impulsivo, desorganizado, sueña dispierto y no puede seguir instrucciones. Quizas tienen dificultad siguiendo las leyes de la sala de clase aunque son muy inteligente y capaz. Despues de eliminar los problemas fisicos y medicos tiene que recibir informacion de la escuela para su doctor para que ellos puedan revisarla con usted. Seria bueno pedir informacion de los maestros, consejeros, y sicologos de la escuela. Quizas ellos o el doctor sugieren un grupo de examenes especiales (Psychomotor, I.Q., Achievement and inventory/checklist para atencion) para cumplir la investigacion.

Cuando toda la informacion esté obtenida quizas esten dirigidos a buscar ayuda en las areas de educacion especial, intervenciones medicas, consejos sicologicos o consejos familiares. Todo esto consejos son para la familia decidir. Es esencial que la escuela y familias trabajen juntos para poder mantener a su hijo en el camino hacia ser un adulto productivo y feliz.

Stephen King, M.D. ha sido un pediatra por 25 años en Atlanta y frequentemente consulta con padres sobre asuntos relativos a la escuela.

How Do Your Feelings Affect Your Learning?

Have you ever had a hard time concentrating because you were excited about weekend plans? Have you ever been distracted by a situation that made you mad, sad, or scared? Whenever you have something going on in your life it causes "big" feelings, your schoolwork can be affected.

All people handle feelings differently. It is important for everyone to pay attention to how different feelings effect them, so that they can cope with their feelings appropri-ately. What is coping? Coping simply means dealing with a situation. Parent and teachers try to teach good coping skills such as under-standing that we all make mistakes, reacting calmly when problems arise, focusing on the positive. Another important coping skill is talking about our feelings with someone we trust like a parent, a friend, or a counselor. Talking about your feelings helps you to get your feelings from your brain out in the open where you can feel understood. This way your brain has more room for learning!

Questions to think about:

What are some feelings that can get in the way of learning?

Who are 3 people you can talk to about your feelings?

I really try but...

Students: Read the paragraphs below written by students who were having a hard time in school.

Paragraph #1:

"School has always been tough for me, but this year is really, really hard. I know that my teachers think I can try better, but things just get confusing for me. There are some kids in my class that seem to have no problem with the work, but I just don't get math. And I like reading, but I seem to take a longer time to read than the kids in my class. I hope people don't think I'm dumb. I don't think I am, it's just that school is sometimes hard for me."

Paragraph #2:

"I get so mad at the other kids who think they are so cool because they are smarter than me. I see them when they laugh at me when I get the wrong answer. I just laugh it off and try not to cry. I know I am really good at things like soccer and music, but school just isn't my thing. I'm good with that, but I wish people would lay off and not look at me when I read slow, or if I don't know the answer. I don't laugh at them when they can't score a goal on the field. Sometimes my embarrassed feelings just build up."

Paragraph #3:

"I just don't care about school. My mom tells me that it's a waste of a good brain. She tells me that I'm lazy, but I don't care. I know that I could ace tests and get good grades if I tried, but why bother? I want to be a professional football player, so why does school even matter? I've had some OK teachers, and this year she's actually really cool. She tells me that I need to have a back up plan in case I get injured and don't get to go to the NFL. She's got a point, but I'll catch up if I need to… right?"

Questions to think about:

Have you ever felt like any of these students?
What feelings do you have while at school?
How do other kids or adults view you as a student?

Chapter 10:

Appendix

Overview:

In this chapter, counselors can see how to prepare for an academic advisement program.

Contents

Documentation

Year_____ ❏ Fall   ❏ Winter   ❏ Spring

_____ participated in Academic Advisement group.
The following methods/strategies were components of this program:

❏ Small Group Work on Study Skills

❏ Visual Organizers

❏ Individual Guidance Sessions on Academic Achievement

❏ Weekly Goal Setting

❏ Positive Reinforcement

❏ Parental Involvement

Counselor Comments:

This documentation can be put in a child's folder of documentation that might be collected through a student support/strategy team that might be looking to help with student success.

CONGRATULATIONS!

You have completed the ACADEMIC ADVISEMENT program!

This certificate is to recognize

for improvement is school success skills.

Signature

Date

Documentation of Test Scores
Pre-Post Group

Student's Name	Pre-Group Score		Post-Group Score	
	Math	Reading	Math	Reading

Group Reunion to Measure
Success/Maintenance

Having a "reunion" meeting approximately a month after academic advisement concludes is a great idea for several reasons. It is a great way to check in with students to measure the continued success, to broaden the sense of belonging to this group, to foster the connections between the students, for the counselor to follow-up with students. This "reunion" will be something that the students will look forward to. Below is a reminder that the counselor can send to the students.

- -

Invitation to an academic advisement reunion

It's time to get together with our academic advisement group reunion! We'll be checking in with how you are doing so make sure you are keeping up with your goals. In preparation for our meeting ask yourself these questions:

Are you:

❏ Keeping your belongings organized?

❏ Working towards your goals?

❏ Avoiding procrastination?

❏ Using stress management techniques?

❏ Studying for tests?

❏ Coming to school on time?

I look forward to getting an update on how you are doing with your academic work!

See you on _____ at _____

in_____.

Your counselor,

References

Brigman, G., & Campbell, C. (2003). Helping students improve academic achievement and school success behavior. *Professional School Counseling, 7*, 91-98.

Gladding, Samuel T. (1998). *Group work: A counseling specialty* (3rd. ed.). Englewood Cliffs, NJ: Merrill.

King, L. (2005). *Making the link: Helping students link school habits with the world of work.* Chapin: SC. YouthLight, Inc